THE WAKING DREAM
39 POEMS
WILLIAM ANDERSON

ex LiBRIS CROSSLEY-holland

THE WAKING DREAM

39 POEMS

WILLIAM ANDERSON

HUTCHINSON
London Melbourne Sydney Auckland Johannesburg

Hutchinson Benham Limited
17/21 Conway Street London W1P 5HL
An imprint of the Hutchinson Group
London Melbourne Sydney Auckland
Wellington Johannesburg and agencies
throughout the world
First published 1983

Designed by Ivan and Robin Dodd
Set in Monotype Photina by
Southern Positives & Negatives (SPAN),
Lingfield, Surrey
Printed in Great Britain by The Anchor Press
and bound by Wm Brendon & Son Ltd,
both of Tiptree Essex

ISBN 0 09 151490 8 Hardback
ISBN 0 09 151491 6 Paperback

CONTENTS

Part One   **OBEDIENCE IN THE HOUSE OF WINDOWS**

  1   Winter wakings: canzone *2*
  2   Prison *4*
  3   Kestrel *5*
  4   The rockmen *6*
  5   Ravenna: Dante's tomb *8*
  6   The connoisseur *9*
  7   Obedience in the house of windows *11*
  8   Fall *12*
  9   Autumn *13*
10   Roads *14*
11   The pilgrims *15*
12   Akbar dies *16*
13   Canzone for a young girl *19*

Part Two   **THE TRIPLE PEAK**

14   A husband to his bride: canzone *22*
15   Freak wave *24*
16   The other men *27*
17   Potters of the T'ang *28*
18   Waiting for the whoosh *29*
19   Dissolution *31*
20   The triple peak *32*
21   Slighted *35*
22   Coming out of gas *36*
23   Why they die *37*
24   Mseilah: the princess of beyond the seas *39*
25   Salamander *41*
26   Sometimes I see you: canzone *46*

Part Three   **PREHISTORY**

27   Canzone for a dead woman   *48*
28   Franz   *49*
29   Patience   *52*
30   Harvest   *53*
31   Lefthand, righthand: another prince,
      another flight   *54*
32   Found   *55*
33   Prehistory   *56*
34   New voice   *57*
35   Beaufort   *58*
36   Your only name   *59*
37   Ambitions   *61*
38   In the room of the tribal gods   *62*
39   St. Sophia: sestina   *71*

NOTE

'The waking dream' of the title of this collection is a phrase that recurs throughout many of the poems. This phrase describes the state of awareness created by the merging of the waking and the dream states. This may also be seen as the union in our experience of the outer physical world and the inner imaginative world. In this state of awareness landscapes may assume an archetypal significance, the most ordinary objects may be charged with meaning, events long separated in time may reveal their inner emotional resemblances, and symbols and images may demand expression in stories. These poems arose from different experiences of the waking dream; their rhythms and forms derive from the mood and emotional nature of these experiences.

Furthermore, the poems are arranged in form, theme, and image, to throw light on one another as varied expressions of this state. They are set out in three parts around the central poem 'The triple peak' which is itself a description of the incursion of the waking dream into the experience of the world of nature. The inner part of this poem is in *canzone* form; poems in variants of the *canzone* form (of which the *sestina* is one) are placed at the beginning and end of each of the three parts. The connexions between the poems are conveyed not only by their placing in the linear sequence but in other ways as well. There is a relationship between each pair of poems as they radiate symmetrically out from 'The triple peak'; thus 'Dissolution' relates to 'Slighted', 'Waiting for the whoosh' relates to 'Coming out of gas', and so on to the first and last poems, 'Winter wakings' and 'St. Sophia'. The collection may be read and regarded as a novel of events in the soul or as a game of subtle connexions. Either way, it is meant to give pleasure.

I am told I must explain the word 'Memnonic' in 'Salamander'; it is not a misprint for 'mnemonic' but my own coining from the Egyptian statue of Memnon which sings when touched by the rays of the sun at dawn.

My thanks are due to Cecil Collins for permission to use his drawing 'Figures in a landscape' in the cover design of the book. 'The potters of the T'ang' first appeared in *Encounter*; an earlier version of 'Salamander' appeared in *Time & Tide*; 'Your only name', 'In the room of the tribal gods', and 'St. Sophia' have also appeared elsewhere.

W.A.

PART I

OBEDIENCE IN THE HOUSE OF WINDOWS

1
WINTER WAKINGS: CANZONE

What lives and catches light or sends
Light lapping like repeated sound
Of birdsong beckoning past the bends
Of paths by copse or forest bound;
What depth that glaze or brushwork lends
To stir in me the burial mound
Of love's long-severed broken ends;
I knew these when the five swans downed,
Flew level where the dyke curved round,
Struck water with their wings to flee
Into the greater white of sun that crowned
The river where it met the sea.

I stand within my room and see
The fall of night and snow together;
The flakes fall down by wall and tree
And cast on me forgotten weather
As out of nowhere comes a cry:
'What sign was put on snow to gather
Such pain and rapture through the eye?'
I bow before the voice and offer
My thoughts surrendered to the Other
Whose one thought falls on mind and land
To test, like plants the snow will smother,
What dies in cold, what few may stand.

Princess, at your command,
The giant who serves you as your slave,
Rammed in my skull his bunched-up hand –
No further sight of himself he gave –
Then forced his fingers to expand
And show by thumb-ball and the line of love
Your gift: an uncut diamond.
No words: its state told well enough;
I must cleave the stone now in the rough
And cut against the crystal grain,
Taking, if need be, all my life
To show, as light, your right to reign.

2
PRISON

A wood laps the edge of its bare sandstone crest.
No convict is allowed the direct light;
The ruling judgment which preceded arrest
Demands that a sentence be passed in night.
The Governor, reckoning faith the best gaoler,
Ordered his raven chaplains to preach
That freedom is acceptance, a will to failure
Which colours the prisoners' thought and speech.
It is small wonder then doubt opens crevasses
In most plausible plans the moment begot.
One cannot escape alone or in masses
Though crowds tunnel and the lonely plot.
The secret is: two or three can escape:
Those who have not let their minds malinger,
Have learned all their warders' quirks and can ape
The face of surveillance, the trigger finger,
And study their prison's moods and time
Till they know the hour one evening in summer
When guards doze through the tower clock's chime.
Up the ramp to the roadblock they saunter
So resembling their warders strolling to beer
No guard checks the uniform or flicks through the passes.
Like government servants, they suffer no fear
Of the trees of the forest to mark their faces.
Kicking the sand up they swing down the road
Till shadows of trunks make a dark intersection,
Then swiftly to the left they leap into the wood,
To water where bloodhounds will lose all direction.
Still in disguise; not until the rising moon
Glitters on swamp ivy and the river willows
When the nightjars and pigeons whistle and croon
Does their laughter burst in muffled billows
And they drop to their sleep on the swathes of bowed rushes,
Three faces resigned to the rule of the night,
Three minds as unworked as the leaves of the bushes,
Keeping till morning new lives, fresh flight.

4

KESTREL

Here where every flower
And leaf has learned to cower,
Where heather, gorse, and thrift
Are tumps upon the cliff,
Where ravens, gulls, and men
Are scattered once again,
Each time they muster force
To set their wanted course,

You lean upon the air
With head bent in one stare,
With flick to wingtip's sail,
Down-arch of feather tail,
And lift and droop of talons
To regulate your balance,
As true to your fixed hover
As though it were fair weather.

You alone can act
So gales do not distract
Your power upon your deed
But turn winds to your need
Of vantage over all;
And should you choose free fall
It is because you will
To stoop upon your kill.

4
THE ROCKMEN

On moorlands, up synclines
Where nearer the summit
The heather recedes
From the crest of sedges,
Leaving shoals of the whortle,
Of harebell in pools,
O at the point of every hill
Which was first of its range
To rise out of sea,

This sad thing, this poor thing
This mirror, this mind
Worn out with language,
Exhausted with thinking,
Stumbles in searching
For points of beginning,
And sinks into half sleep
On the sharp rattling grasses.

Then after rest, in sudden awakening you come to
See the high wethers, the hill tumps, the rockmen,
Welling from soil that was ground from their brothers,
The weak ones, the faulted, whom glaciers and rainstorms
Crushed and eroded;
And you wonder in fear
'How did I miss them? Were they here when I came?'
Check your map. Sometimes they're marked,
But often surveyors were blind as their tools,
And then you relax, finding comfort in musing
On how they endure, on the way they wipe clean
The mind that regards them to their own mere reflection
Of dry light, of cloud-shape, and of sun after rain.

Three heads under the one sky.

Three drunken hermits in a storm.

Three hooded women who disdain
To bare their beauty to the common eye
Or spell their secrets to the air.

Beware their heads!
Or make yourself be strong.
Whatever way you look at them
An eye wakes up and beams
Through your existence,
A singing starts within your ear,
And every molecule of air
Is made to dance
As you now dance.
'Fool, fool' their whispers run
'You think you have a mind
But if we chose we could transmit
A thought that would explode your skull,
A heart-beat that would melt your bones,
Laughter to vaporize your lungs,
And tears to turn you into steam'.
And dangerously they start to laugh
With thunder in their sunken roots,
Stopping because they do not care.

And in their silence show such power
You could imagine they chose Earth to sleep
And need a denser planet when they dance
Whirling there with comet tails, exulting
In superstitious dread their flight evokes.

5
RAVENNA: DANTE'S TOMB

Cypresses: a cloister scrawled with messages,
One bigger than the rest: 'Power
To the imagination'; but who, before the hour
When bronze gates swing back with a clanged report,
Could imagine from these presages
The peace Pietro Lombardi made to flower
In Dante's face as, at the window of a tower,
He turns from book to book to weigh a thought.

Here exile, iron cliffs, fear of flame, all cease;
The sculptor's art incises every page,
Returns to the poet what his labours made:
Joy of the Renaissance, the escalade
Of liberty up to the ladder's highest stage
Where her smile made eternal his release.

6
THE CONNOISSEUR

So busy is the connoisseur,
(Rich and born with taste),
He had to call the agents in
To make his large collection grow.

Out they scurry through the shops,
Their eyes agleam with five-per-cents,
And stagger back with *sang-de-boeuf*,
With Rembrandts dated, duly signed;

The last Uccello in private hands
Is his, a cable wings:
But once within his private hall,
Returned from many months away,

He winces at the paltry daubs,
The modern watermark inlaid,
The suspect craquelure, the peel
Of curled veneer from pink new wood,

And has the hall cleared out at once,
Leaving perhaps some slipware there,
Three pewter mugs, a tile with charm,
Square dust-marks where the frames had hung.

And who's to blame?
He has the taste to make his choice;
No agents, no vicarious flair,
Can weld his knowledge with his love.

And he has far more left than I
When after such an absence gone,
I call to book my licensed eyes,
My ears empowered, my sanctioned heart,

And catalogue their recent gains;
Rejecting each against the test
'What thought in that is mine?
What feeling is not borrowed?'

7

OBEDIENCE IN THE HOUSE OF WINDOWS

The grey-haired mirrors in their age
Forget what's present or what's past,
Revisit childhood when the image
Of a parent portrait near is glassed
Before me. A lake exhales a mist
And this house, loving light with windows,
Fanlights, ox-eyes, candle twist,
Must be obedient to the weather's throes.

A poplar leaf, spinning on the tree,
Is flashed from glass to glass and back
Through Argus-eyed asymmetry –
Sinking in velvet folds of black.
A sunburst breaks from the white-edged cloud,
The trees lash their boughs in greeting,
The mirrors wake with a forest bowed,
With leaves and light in meeting.

Once hating the house's age and strength
For taking us too for changing moods,
Content I walk this gallery's length
Knowing I'm part of it, one of its foods,
And in content my mind expanding
Learns what the house knows day and night,
Encompassing each room and landing,
Obedient to the thrusts of light.

8
FALL

In uplands, in highlands, old women are praying
In a cool dark church through which light slanting
Inflames the paint on the blood-streaming body
Of Christ in agony nailed to the cross.
Their lips are muttering, their rosaries clicking
As they offer in sacrifice their sins, their lives,
Their children lost, and their hopes destroyed.
But one after one sees a shaft of the sun
Impose another face onto the mask
And they hear as a thought the words of the face:
'I did not suffer as you thought I suffered.'
'My love was not given for you to despair.'
The vault resounds with a crack as the arms
Split from the body and swing on the nails
And the worm-eaten torso thumps on the altar
And clatters to rest, dripping frass on the stones.
The women rush to the door in terror
And scream at the silent square in their rage,
Cursing the sun for the lives they wasted,
Kicking the earth because they were born –
All except one who remains prostrated,
Calm with her thanks for the space left empty.

9
AUTUMN

The grapes hang down to the lake
That swells their bloom in its glass;
The morning glories take
From sky and mountain face
Their blue.

I feel rich autumn arise –
All autumns I have known;
And, as you sit, your eyes
Reflect from rinded flesh and stone
The dew.

You also bring to birth
But make a hidden thrift,
Till cold is on the earth,
A child, a gift
In you.

ROADS

By which I must mean
Lanes where you walk down the middle
Without a car knocking you down –
Lanes that keep all day
The slug tracks made at night,
Whose hedges whiskered with hay
Caught from carts like fat old women,
Weep soil on the tarmac;
And at the point the lane goes out of sight
Whether on a crest or edge of shade,
That meeting of unseen and seen,
That feather touch of hope,
Has now so often pierced my heart
I find them made continuous in my mind.

One where a chaffinch sang
The first phrase of a Glinka overture
Is edited onto –
Snip go the cutter's scissors; off
Fall reels of years and miles –
Another road bordered by pools
With sticklebacks in the linking stream.
Telegraph poles from Scotland to the West
Join in this geography
With no intermittent Kingdom;
Their voices sing or fall silent
With rapid change of weather;
Silent at the crossroads where
The contemplation of the sun on earth
Makes urgency of choice illusion.

Who cut the film to make this road,
Creating from fragments of existence
A path for one new life?
I only know the hidden pilgrim finds
The sacred way made plain
In a lightning flash of grace.

11
THE PILGRIMS

They know where they are and where they are going.
At certain times one can watch them pass
Over this great knobbled plain of grass
Where their one companion, the wind, is blowing.

See! in the distance the black form of their train
Bends into the bowl of a hollow;
Then up, unwound by the road they follow,
They come nearer to us and nearer again.

I do not know what is the goal of their faith;
They use this road and I come to see them,
Hoping a blessing or thought will flee them
And change to an angel a weather-torn wraith.

Fall on your knees as they pass. We are food
For their prayers and our land is theirs.
The cloud transforms the water it bears:
Long grasses glitter in the sun's bright mood.

None of them talks. The only noise, a pipe
Played by their leader skirls in the air
A forbidding tune, emphatic and bare
Like the whirl of plover and call of snipe.

The plain still pines with their pipe; and blowing,
The wind out-chases them over the hill.
And we are deprived here unknowing still
Where they may be and where they are going.

12
AKBAR DIES

The falcon churns the air above
The pointed domes and watered courts,
Arcades, and galleries to the room
Where Akbar slowly dies.

The conversations on one faith
That packed his court are silent now:
The brahmin leaders have withdrawn;
The mullahs and ulemas sleep.

Alone two Jesuits wait and eye
The naked blades that guard the door,
Fingering crosses under cloaks
And hissing in their muted quarrel:

'The guards will stop us breaking in.
He cannot read a note. We wait' –

'And while we wait, he dies
When India could be ours!
If he receives us, he is saved!
If we are killed, a martyrdom!' –
'But when he dies, suppose his son
Acknowledges Christ's Church?
To lose that by unseemliness!' –

Their whispers splutter, sullen lamps
Swing slowly in the gusts of heat
That hardly stir long veils of gold.

Perhaps their whispers penetrate,
Perhaps he remembers one more sect
That took imperial courtesy
As evidence they'd won his soul.

*   *   *

The falcon ceases wheeling, stops
In air and hovers with
Her wingtips tingling,
Gaze entire:

And stillness falls on India,
Upon the chamber and the bed,
On bowls of seaweed jade
And jade the colour of the moon,
And pearls that scattered from his robe:
The stillness that he ached for, found
And lost in empire, conquest, war,
Returns with savour of his every deed:
The stillness of the scent of dawn,
The squirrel in the plane tree leaves
That watched the tiger by its trunk,
The horsetail standards raised to charge,
The match and cannon smoke, the breath
Before his lips met lips
At night time when the wild deer stared,
The pause of judgment, wretched eyes,
The honeycombing of an arch, the smile
Of men who did not need debate
To know the dewdrop from the sea:
All moments that were still in life
Arise and meet
As though the levels of all waters
Rose
And every fountain-laden pond
Spread out to greet
The spilling marble sluices and expand
Through gardens, valleys, and dry plains
Where Indus and the Ganges flood
And where the sea sinks India
In unity beneath his thought.

But in this stillness his dry lips
Are moving, pouting, gasping, striving
Always to repeat one word:
The mercy of the name of God

          *   *   *

The falcon of the Self has stooped
Upon the prey of life and soars
Away to find her home and tear
The soul from flesh with razor claws.

CANZONE FOR A YOUNG GIRL

Now you are in the garden.
                              Look!
Each birch is like a trembling girl
Still frightened though the rains have stopped
But you are not afraid.
                              Suppose
That from the red rose head you shook
The rainbeads on each petal's curl
And in the lifeline of your palm you cupped
The drops that are all soul of rose.

You touch them with your tongue. Scent throws
From brain to limbs prophetic power.
The petals can break off and die
And you'll not mind for you know why
That what is dead is not the flower –
Just as a woman smiles and knows

That time which ruins beauty, health,
May not attack her ground of self.

The garden is so full of loves,
Of tendrils round your fingers, webs
Unseen till on your face, views
You could ponder till you die,

Of boughs plumped with full-breasted doves,
Of gall-wasps laying rusty eggs,
Of peacock butterflies, and the crews
Of rooks a-sail in trees mast-high.

'What do you want from life? Reply!'

The voice will grow to make a wind
That blasts your face and overwhelms
House, mother, father, standing elms
Till every root and leaf is spinned
While you pass through the whirlwind's eye,

And flame-wings make each branch a bird
Beneath whose flights you cry unheard.

It needs response, returns to test
All future loves, each home or rest,
But forges, O my dear, in anguish
Refinement of the one desire
Whose just expression alone has language
To calm and quench the question's fire.

PART II

THE TRIPLE PEAK

14
A HUSBAND TO HIS BRIDE:
CANZONE

This is the last of my lands I show you,
The one I most fear and hold from view,
Keeping secret my love for its clear
Unreasoned power to remain so dear.

I warn you of it; there are places
Where, muttering in all its twigs and shoots,
The forest comes alive with twilight shimmering
And monsters with horned faces
Creep from liquid ashtree roots,
Crawling towards you with eyelids glimmering;
A house that hated each one of its owners,
With windows that smell of dead butterfly wings,
Absorbs you into an old dark obsession
Where you join sad ghosts in a dance upon strings;
Or where simply the shift of an endless grey cloud,
Brushing a hill-top's rounded corners,
Evokes in you loathing, holds your heart cowed,
As barren of choice as its own dull progression.

But some places welcome; barns and granges;
Beaches where the long sea ranges
Over ammonites curled in a bed of stone;
And clumps of oak in the moon full grown.

There, after days spent in heat, you will find
A ruined cottage alone in a wood –
Paneless its windows, broken its door –
Which, sensing you walk among trees as a friend,
Unclenches itself like a chestnut in bud,
Grows again rafters, tiles, and the floor,
And sends candle flicker from china to stairs
Which you will mount, remembering each tread,
Into a room where the perrywinkles twine
Round the tree posts of a leaf-valanced bed
Where we will dream of black and white horses
Coming to drink from a river in pairs
And where, waking, we know the stars in their courses
Unite us with silence as with the one wine.

FREAK WAVE

The hottest day for years. The tide
Has sunk so low it seems evaporated:
Anemones like globs of meat
Gleam through crackling seaweed on the rocks.
Black rocks, white sand, brown bodies.
A woman stirs to loose her straps,
Pouting as she lifts her head,
And bares the half moons of her breasts.
The fellow beside her lies as after
Making love, his belly hot on sand.
A boy is wandering up the beach,
Kicking the tidemark as he looks
For tellin shells. Transistors wail
Like gnats beside each couple.
The sea has gone so far that air
Has taken over water. They feel
As though in deep hot baths. Bubbles
Of heat make grassy dunes
And bush and hazel on the cliffs
Wobble in their gaze.
                              And now
A man gets up to look around,
To see the sails like cabbage butterflies
In mating flight. He turns unguardedly
Towards the sun
                    and drops
To cup his eyes while bloody images
Leap through his head with pain.
A voice resounds throughout his skull:

'Chronos has fallen;
                    his son has unmanned him.
Who heard the splash
                    of bleeding flesh
Fall from a clear sky,
                    sink between waves?'

The man wakes up and looks about.
'O God, I'm mad' he groans
For nothing moves except the lice
That hop in ruts of sand, or towels
That flap like prayer flags on the dunes,
Or falls of dry sand on the crests
That bare white roots of marram grass.

'Chronos has fallen',
                    the voice is behind him.
His shadow is speaking,
                    'Run! you must run!'

He grabs his towel and, sobbing with fright,
Sprints between the legs and arms,
And does not stop until he gains
A mound from which he sees with fear
A nest of foaming in the sea.

The sperm has fermented
                    earth under water.
With heaving and bubbling
                    a wave lashes up
And curls down the beach
                    like a knife unsheathed.
Larger waves break out
                    and roar in the sand drag.
A mother arises,
                    gathers her children,
Then settles down,
                    puzzled, embarrassed
As the sea grows silent,
                    the sun still burns.
Then out of flatness
                    a fifty foot breaker,
Ribbed like a whale,
                    blacks out the sunlight,

Backspraying the sails
                    of overturned dinghies,
Heaves to an arching
                    which muffles the screaming
And thumps on the beach
                    crushing the bathers.
The man on the sand dune
                    sees through his terror
The crest of the breaker
                    bound and rebound
Till cracks in the coastline,
                    forking like lightning,
Cast off the headlands
                    with dolphin-like bellies
And rumbles of earthslide
                    resound in the valleys.
Then as the foaming
                    grows gentle, subsiding,
He watches with wonder
                    a woman now walking,
A woman all naked,
                    her hair bespattered,
With water peeling,
                    a cocoon off her thighs,
Step on the shoreline
                    with unconcerned purpose
And as she passes
                    the broken bodies
Crushed into pits
                    by the force of the wave
The walls cave in on them,
                    leaving a smoothness.
She walks to the sand dune
                    and disappears inland.
The sun is as bright
                    as before her coming
And clouds of white doves
                    are the only clouds seen.

16
THE OTHER MEN

When allowed to stop its fervour
A tired body sits at rest,
The shadow bodies leap from torpor,
From the limbs in which they're pressed:

These other men I feel them only
Such a little way beyond
The skeleton they leave so lightly –
Swallow shadows on a pond –

Feel the first spring, not the landing,
Have to guess the svelte sensation
Of walking through the walls and standing
Poised for yet more levitation

Till with lightning in their sprint-starts
They return to home and kingdom,
To their mothers, to their sweethearts,
And celebrate their secret freedom.

17
POTTERS OF THE T'ANG

They need no words for, if they wish
To utter forms that burn for birth,
They throw, fire, cool their pots,
And meet
In silence when with bows,
With hands outstretched
That deprecate their own or show
Their pleasure at another's work,
They offer and accept their gifts,
Then sit to contemplate
The language of the rounded shape,
The grammar of its line, the vowels
Of glaze in phrase of craquelure,
So that the tacit meaning acts
Upon their minds,
Contracts to specks of black,
Collapsars that engulf all seeing
In eating up the space around,
Or hints in sheaves of light
At nebulae beyond the glimpse
Of other shapes they half-suggest,
A range of mountain tops
Or branches hooped with weight of snow.

WAITING FOR THE WHOOSH

Sunlight falls through hazel wands
To this high Tuscan hill and gleams
On wet black rocks, lamping the pond's
Khaki bottom and escaping streams,

As I work on, priming the pipe
That fails to give us baths or drink,
Work in ignorance but with hope
That soon with a belch the flow will sink;

And as I work, my mind half-dulling
Notes how a frog slips low beneath
A flotilla of pondskaters sculling
Past the brown filagree of one dead leaf;

Housed in the bark of last year's twigs,
A heap of caddis larvae wobbles,
Each clambering on the others' backs,
Staring with eyes like anchored bubbles;

And for a moment I become
Transparent to the sunlight's grace,
My talking thoughts made gladly dumb
At wafted, given happiness;

The hill turns inside out; I seem
Here on its slope, deep in its stone,
Poised in another's waking dream
With whose new consciousness alone

I rise through hairs of every root
Intruded through the rock; I prove
The sap in each incipient shoot
And imprint of each wild boar hoof

As though I were a finer air
Through which a subtler light may pass
To dead and living creatures there,
Changed themselves to permeable glass.

The greater mood overrides the task,
Easing the ache of my employment;
The only charge it has to ask
Is my enjoyment.

With two hopes now I wait the time
When, freed of blocks, drained of self-will,
The pipe sucks down the mounting prime
And water joins the house to hill.

19
DISSOLUTION

Rains in high summer on woods
Voice the need of the soul for dissolution;
If not now, then the chance of
Living beyond the tight boundaries
Of skeleton, flesh and the skullcap,
Not in violence of shipwreck or car-smash,
But steadily seeping and changing
Through the cycle of water streaming
Down the columnar trunks of the beeches,
Leaving no underleaf dry from the drenching;
And the leaves with their own transpiration
In the closeness and heat of the woods
Send up their answering steam
To the constant downfalling of rain.

THE TRIPLE PEAK

The white magnolia flowers in cups:
Its petals fall and, lanced by twigs,
Make sails of flesh with spider rigs.
A scarlet tulip arches back:
The wind makes play with it and taps
Black pollen with a wicked scent,
While cherries stand with hands upbent
To scatter blossom on the track.

Some leaves are born the purple-brown –
Virginia creeper, roses, oak –
They'll wear at death in autumn smoke,
But what excites the wind is green!
The beech leaves open, fleeced with down,
Heave into sunlight and then plunge
Like foam beneath the next wave's lunge
And rise, tempestuously serene.

But that's in one world only.
When two worlds meet, my Janus faces
Explore at once their mirrored spaces.
I know I'm in this room, I know –

        I stand upon the flinty road,
        High on the pass, hot in the sun,
        And see the course this road will run
        Though hid by valleys, marches;

        But still it mounts their depths straight bored
        Through lizard crests of rounded banks,
        Etches the higher shadowed flanks
        And flares by tower and broken arches,

Till over every height it reaches
The mountain of the triple peak
And hides upon those shoulder ends
Where from the blue ravines it sends,
Back through the shafts of light that streak
Into a single ray that bleaches

The interval of air with fire,
Renewal to my one desire.

Though in other mountains hung with pall
Of clouded stars or snowbright days,
Swifter and deeper than cosmic rays
Time eats their great foundations through,

Here vibrance of the voice whose call
Pitched fuming clusters into flame,
Stirred dust to give man form and name,
Sustains this as the day it grew;

And, as I see the mountain's blue,
All fear of time to come takes cover
For in my mind the angel stands,
Silver and gold cups in his hands,
And pours from each cup to the other
The waters of the old and new

Over which smile his burning eyes
At laughter in eternal skies.

The three worlds part – lonely,
Powerless at the point they sever,
I wait for storms and wilder weather
To blow them back as they now go.

The children fight against the wind
A mile along the winter beach
Until the headland comes in reach
And then they turn, outspread their hands,
Their hair all flustered and unpinned,
And sail on tiptoe up the shore,
Their shouts unheard above the roar
Of waves expanding on the sands.

A little while, a little while,
They give their bodies to the breeze,
Delighted to be so at ease,
As trusting to the powers of force
As all the particles that whirl,
With wind and earth and galaxy,
In air or in vacuity,
And stop –
                    bewildered, hoarse.

21
SLIGHTED

You with your scorn
Besieged my antique fortress,
You shelled my curtain walls,
Filled in the moat,
And in the very keep of which I boasted
As impregnable, you planted
Not your standards but
Placards with messages of hate,
While having in control
The slighting of my crenellations.

So made a peasant
In a modern world,
Without a bundle left
I issued penniless

To find a bungalow,
A suburb hemmed
With sterile cherry trees,
Where hidden among houses still
I write

My praises of you,
Not
As the world's first woman president,
But as my queen.

22
COMING OUT OF GAS

Couched on Olympus, I experience
The white limbs, the glorious, the gold
Hair of the goddesses as airs that enfold
A grove of trees – no division
Of world and self breaks the coherence
Of my full happiness; my heart
Makes a cup hollowed to hold, impart,
Ambrosia; my mind one clear vision
Of waves meeting sunlight with gleams and nods
Ringed by heroes, the goddesses, the gods.

Ringed by my friends, I now explain
Life on Olympus; the longer I talk
The grimmer their brows, the more they baulk,
And the absurdity of trying to express
The ineffable bursts like the main
Of a cosmic joke whose fountains roll
Drowning all words in delight of the soul.
I can't stir my coffee, aim spoon and miss:
The very sight of them so unbelieving
Rocks me with laughter, sets my body heaving.

Heaving with laughter, I open my eyes:
The blood streams down my tongue and chin;
The grimy bathroom glass lets in
Wet sunlight; the worried dentist snaps –
As my laughter wakes even his surprise –
Just like a nanny, 'Calm down, that's enough.
Calm down' – as though he were the stuff
Of calmness and I were close to collapse.
But I am sane as gods; he took a tooth;
I rob his surgery of Olympian youth.

WHY THEY DIE

Musk set a pattern of a kind –
In the twenties –
When it withdrew its scent,
In a huff perhaps
Though no one knows,
Leaving its flowers to nod by becks,
Redolent only in name.

But that had nothing of the *gravitas*,
The majestic sulk of the elms
When they decided to go,
Like senators, fixing on
The subtle means of death:
A synthanatic use
Of beetle and a fungus.

Creaking with sardonic boughs
As they anticipated
All the letters to the *Times*
Giving all reasons but the right one
Why they died;
Amused at man's bewildered love
Of their great forms,
Their cumuli of leaves by day
Mounting like anchored clouds
Or thunder-bearing anvils;
And at night
Salutations to the Queen of Darkness,
Deeper blacknesses imposed upon the dark;
They spoke as one in one great voice
And said:
'Well may you love us
But the love that looks and does not use
Our bodies for the works of men
Is empty, vain, and fruitless.

For centuries since the Romans brought us
We held the water round our roots
That fed the grasses and the corn
In fields our leafage bordered,
Making your labour fruitful;
And for after work
We gave you rest
In seats of chairs
And arms that gained their polish
From hands long used to soothe
The cross-grain of our annual rings;
And then the longest rest
In coffins joined of our planks and boards.

We do not feel the needful axe;
We have not been renewed;
We have taken umbrage.–
Away!'

And so they go.
For several summers they'll remain
Like unleafed winter trees
And then they'll crumble;
Their best remembrance
In oils and watercolours
As painful to behold
As shafts and roofless naves of
Monasteries dissolved
Because the labour and the prayer
No longer made men Man.

And they have left
The infection of displeasure
To beech and sycamore,
To oak and thorn,
Who even now in conclave waver
On whether to adopt their doom.

MSEILAH: THE PRINCESS OF
BEYOND THE SEAS

The sky could be her face down bent
Upon this clover-laden plain
Where oval gorge and peaks above
Enclose an orange-flower scented space,
A landscape of what in the brain
Protects the hidden seat of love.

There's only one way in; the track
Leads upstream through a high defile
Hung with scrub and cavern brink
And joins, where the river doubles back,
A bridge you pass in single file,
Whose cobbles mule-hoof polished pink.

Past citrus groves their leaves have topped,
The poplars wave like welcoming hands
Beyond the river, shallow, full,
That broadens where, with height abrupt,
An island in the flat green lands,
The rock presents a giant's skull;

A skull that wears a crown of gold,
A castle calm in evening light
Whose dark rockface beneath recalls
Those bearded heads by springs who told
To travellers words of limbic blight,
Of journey's wreck and fated falls.

But, once we're up, blood dreams find ease
In chambers of the castle crown,
Which, empty to the eye, insist
The Princess of beyond the seas
Is of the air, is here to drown
All fear within her healing kiss.

She's there as quick as scent of flowers,
Makes seconds gleam like fountain froth,
Rewards the arduous pilgrimage
With tents of silk on shaded towers,
Gardens of brimstone flight and moth,
Blue pimpernel and crimson sage . . .

But with descent the world returns;
The students clap and stamp their feet;
Fat ladies scold their toddling sons;
Drivers reverse; a dust cloud churns
And from the gorge quick shots repeat
As small birds fall to hunters' guns.

SALAMANDER

Three masters since the work began
Had tamed an element to make it serve
The growing of the young cathedral:
Foundations of the ox of earth
Spread like tree roots through the ground:
The fish of water taught the stone
To flow in fountains of the columns
And kelp and seawrack traceries;
The eagle of the air spread wings
In fine-boned vaults: the counterpoise
Of hover in a clash of thermals.

Now time brought close the hardest risk:
The need for fire to show how gravity
Could further be defied in towers
To lead the souls of regions round
Through mountain paths of yes and no
To bell-resounding spires.

The weather suited this next job:
The wind drove clouds without a break,
Hung raindrops on each sainted nose,
Then blew them off in curving gouts
That splashed the puddles in the square.
The masons formed a palisade
To hedge the salamander round,
Giving it wary space.

Its body still, its tail in tremor,
It moved its head in puzzlement:
Eyes burning with black opal lights
Searched for theirs and baulked their gaze.
It howled
In desperation for the life of fire;
The vaulting shuddered with its cry;
The men
Looked for each other's terror at the thought
The building of a hundred years would crash
In resonance of a higher shriek.

The master of the works, the fourth in line,
Placed hand upon its lizard neck,
And whispered in its ear.
That done, he orderd up his squads.
Like bee-wings on a darkened comb,
Their leather jerkins dully shone
In mounting up from niche to niche;
The quarter-logs of ladders thrummed
With nimble climbing and the crane
Swung out between the squat west towers.
The salamander still kept quiet
And showed no fight as others cowered
Beneath its belly, wound the wads
And tackle for the rope,
And, when they'd finished, sprang away
To let their master climb upon
The salamander's back and stand,
One hand to grasp the central rope,
The other free to wave
A signal to the windlass men.
Then man and monster rose in air
Through constant shadow with a gentle sway
And, as they hung at ordered halts,
Which was the conquered none could tell.

The crane had raised them
To a third its height above the ground
When vehemently a gust of sun
Sent shark-like gleamings through the square,
Set cobblestones and pools ablaze
And caught the salamander's eyes.
It shrieked and lurched;
Men on ladders fended it with brooms;
Plunging its head it ripped the tackle,
Twisted to hurl its rider off,
Swung out in growing circles,
A pendulum in rhythm with its rage.
The crane stopped pulling;
The master shouted new commands
And masons in the shadows sang
So every voussoir, niche, and hole
Made lips of mouths for music,
Memnonic in the wind of song,
And as they all were singing, so
The oscillations dwindled down,
The salamander dropped its head,
Obedient to its master's will,
Till, at the cranehead, men with hooks
Grappled it to a hanging shelf.

At the crossing they let it sleep.
The master posted men to watch
From various quarters of the roof.
At night they brought up braziers, set
Them round the beast and, in response,
A slow light flickered in its flesh
Which woke into a steady glow.
They watched it rise upon its haunches,
Shed a sheath of flame that ran
Amongst their feet and settled

In squares and circles where the towers should climb,
And, as it rose to stand, more skins
And veils of fire sloughed from its sides
As slow as apple boughs to ash,
Then flew to build the flaming walls
That grew around it on the central crossing
And in the towers of front and transept.
With timed precision next, its wings
Spread out and with wide beats
Flung scales of flame through darkness
Which stood in torchlike finials
Or laced the night with buttresses of fire
And hung upon the watchers' heads,
Winged tongues of language they must comprehend
To manifest the new.

Its flesh surrendered to the towers of fire,
The salamander, now a skeleton
Lined within its walls of flame,
Bent back its skull, and thrust
Its wing bones upwards
And vanished in a gale of fire
That in a roar completed
The flambeau of the central spire.
The watchers' tears of gratitude
Were turned to steam by heat
As now the great cathedral sailed
The waves of blackness through the night,
An ark of fire set true on course
Above the drowning centuries.

For miles around men woke from sleep,
Stared from their cottage doors and wept,
Thinking the world would end.
And only those whom art had trained
So to concentrate upon the deed
They had no time to be afraid,
Could watch and note and make secure

In memory that, what the fire
Had built, their stone should emulate.
The master of the works
Felt something die within him;
He prayed and spoke in bidding loud
His dead predecessors' names,
Knowing them present with him;
His fellows spoke his own
Within their hearts where triumph
Of success so long desired, so long
To reach fruition, still remained
An underglow before the vision
That made the night less dark in fading,
Wisped to the faintness of the stars.

SOMETIMES I SEE YOU:
CANZONE

Sometimes I see you;
      you walk under trees,
Your hair taking fire
      in the shafting of sun;
Or else at a window
      when a storm has begun,
All peace
      as the panes shake and quiver;

Or again among people
      talking at ease,
I see your whole life
      as you stop still and turn
And afloat in your eyes
      are the questions that burn:
Flames
      for the dead on a river;

And then I reflect:
      it is not that we dream
But that we are the ones
      who are dreamed, my lover,
By a mind beyond ours
      quite different, quite other,
Awake when it dreams,
      self-contented, supreme.

And in the dark future,
      gleam the eyes of grandchildren;
Hear them whisper aloud,
      'They exist, they are there!'
And the hand that has knotted
      our lives in the pattern
Is reaching for them,
      is poised in the air.

PART III

PREHISTORY

CANZONE FOR A DEAD WOMAN

O celebrator of the sun,
Death has laid a mask of gold
On all you lived and all you told
In long and ringing rhymes;

You heard the threads of silence run
Below the earth, above the sky
And knew beyond man's bitter cry
The praise of other climes.

All resonance of sound and chimes
Would gladden you with crusted light;
You saw the minerals' heaving fight
To grow, to flower in future times;

And in the stars you made us know
The hawthorn branches hung with snow

Go gladly then to meet your dead:
The gilded heroes in the dark;
The girls who wander in the park;
The tutors and the maids;

The summers when great-grandmother said
'Every tale I tell you grows
Into a house, a face, a rose;
None in a poem ever fades'.

The sibyl of the Earth unbraids
Her hair and longs to die;
The sibyl of the Sun throws high
The butterfly from caverned shades.

Go gladly then; you saw the whole
Like sunlight in a golden bowl.

FRANZ

Why do I find you in a dream,
Franz, you burly Prussian,
Dead ten years ago?
Like a round robin about your face,
Every story that you told
Writes a signature to your life
Making the dream an epitaph.

Before the war a monumental mason,
You specialized in marble slabs
For cinema foyers in East Prussia.
Once at a masked carnival,
You danced with the finest woman there.
How your fingers waggled,
Describing her figure and your hopes!
At midnight the dancers all unmasked
And she
Was 'old, so old!'

On cold nights you remembered Stalingrad;
A staff car driver, you were lucky
But you couldn't forget
The woman with her breasts cut off
Dying in a valley with the shells coming over;
Nor forget the night when, sent out to observe,
You lay in snow on a hill brow,
And something big came down;
You rolled away, then back
To staring through your glasses,
But, from the corner of your eye,
You noticed a black shape spread out
Upon the snow around you –
Your blood. The cold of Stalingrad
Anaesthetized the shrapnel wound.
Telling the story,

You whipped your shirt up to display
The scar that flared across your huge back's width.

You bore luck on your back; flown
To Germany on one of the last planes
Out of the Russian encirclement,
Patched up, you fought again.
Running along a dyke in Holland,
Your men behind you in the dawn –
Sheets of white water on either side –
You met some English soldiers.
Each patrol was running to the other
With hands raised in surrender;
The only quarrel between you was
Which side should be the prisoners,
An argument you won.

Ex-POW, you won esteem
For your industriousness,
Labouring for Cornish farmers.
You found a wife,
Her face a cider apple – but at least
You knew that from the start.
The only time regret
Passed through your eyes
Was when we played your favourite 78,
Heimweh mit dir.
Where was home?
And who was she?
But what was more your nature than regret
Showed in your vigour
As you humped sacks
Or hurtled to a pub,
Talking always with German consonants
And Cornish vowels, exclaiming
'O my tear soul!'

O my dear soul, friend
Now acknowledged as a friend
In ways I was too young then to accept,
In dreams we pay our depts of feeling,
Debts to friendship undervalued,
And this dream balances the book
With what was constant in you:
You had the gift of living in the present
That kept you free of lies about the past
And what made homes for you in every passing moment
Was the calm that underlay your vigour,
Filling your life
As your great frame would fill a room.

PATIENCE

A grey wind blows
The horsepond surface;
Each lazy ripple grows
Wider on its journey southwards
To lapse on stones wth a tired grate.
Gloomed as by night,
Two frogs embracing
Leave and re-enter sight
In a ripple's passing
Over the weed tops where they mate.

His forelegs clutch
Her larger body:
They sway together with such
Currents as make the weeds shudder,
Abase their fronds and lift.
Her left paw up-
Twists in surrender
Its white webs to a fluted cup,
Making a gesture so tender,
Just watching her bestows a gift.

Otherwise
They do nothing.
The clouded skies
And water under the wind's scuffing
Bend my thoughts to the dreaming earth
So that I resign
My quarrel with the day's inertia
And comprehend its sign
As the intrinsic pleasure
Known in the pause before a birth.

30
HARVEST

Scent of seven sisters' rose:
The honey moon swings high and fills
Acres of the standing wheat
With shadows thrown from ear and hair
And glisters down each silent stalk.
As quiet as bloom on swelling plums
She ripens softness in the sky;
And here, behind, I know you wait,
Love perpetual, with your scythe
To win this silence to your store.

LEFTHAND, RIGHTHAND:
ANOTHER PRINCE, ANOTHER
FLIGHT

Billy the Butcher is riding the hills,
In sweetness of anger, with purpose unfogged;
His soldiers spread out through the heather like weals
As though the whole land were a back he has flogged.

And high on the cols the starved women moan
With stench of burnt thatch fouling the air
As they look down to crossroads where gallow trees groan
With the ripening harvest of men that they bear.

But a red-haired girl takes an uncharted route,
Steps first of her party through a white-rocked stream,
And always eludes the straight lines of pursuit
As though words were their hunters and she a dream.

Kilted as her servant or prinked out as her maid,
The fugitive follows her, striding along,
With no fear in her presence of being betrayed,
His heart grown the master of grief and of wrong.

Where once he'd be lost, he learns to provide;
He wears his fate like a fine-hammered ring;
No more a pretender with her image his guide,
He knows what to rule, what it is to be king.

Like lovers in flight, up green mountains in silence
They bear with them kingship crowned by her grace
Over the headlands that thread out to islands
Where the lashing of waves gives promise of peace.

The dreams that have led them to freedom and glory
Are nightmares to Billy in palace and town,
Still threatening his rule in song and in story
That drums and the squeak of his fifes cannot drown.

32
FOUND

We were out hunting for the hidden man,
Posted scouts, dragged the country bare;
Some thought that they had glimpsed him
But descriptions clashed. Reports flowed in
Which diligently we filed if ever
We spared time from the search.
Each mountain, bank of lake, and wood
Was threaded by our watching men.
All this seemed more than useless –
Yet one day
While we patrolled an open plain
With alders sunk beside their streams
And hardly cover for the hares,
There he was,
Running and our way,
Kicking up a wake of pollen,
Shouting as though we were old friends.
He greeted us as warmly as the sun;
We felt so happy just to meet him
We forgot to be reserved, to doubt;
The happiness itself is proof.

PREHISTORY

Out of the grey, the ancestral sea,
They are dragging the past out of me.

Spread up the slipway they wait for the sign
And heave in the slack of the tautening line.

Flopped on the planking slumps a beast;
It lifts a head long thought deceased;

A turtle-like head with homeless black eyes;
The rope still tugs at it where it lies;

And I regard its mussel-blue legs
Fading to white and steely pegs;

The matted hairs where each limb joins
The casing of its fortressed loins;

The rounded chest that its ribs engrave
Built for the pressure of an undersea wave.

Out of the grey, the night time sea,
They have dragged the past out of me,

And all I can do is to call it my own,
Push by the people to whom it is shown,

See their eyes judge what is clear in my heart,
'What stopped its growth here must make a new start';

And hug the wet carcass with tears and regret
For its greater fellows still to home on me yet.

NEW VOICE

Wait for the new voice!
The old words die and rot
But the sounds return from the time
When Adam gave names to beasts
With bugle vowels in Eden.

Then see the crumbling of Jerichos,
Foundation on foundation of lies,
Till under, as in you, you find
A truth all had laboured to hide.

Like sun to glass, it flashes
Into fountains which gush out
And drown our feeble thoughts.
Then love is seen in the hated
And the tear is known to be false.
Call on the voice; only it can still
The revenge of the waiting soil,
Ashes of forests and plains destroyed,
And sunken faults in the grieving mountains.

To our inflammable dryness
Shall come its late spring thunder,
Signalling the healing sap
To rise and burst the buds.
Then man will return to the peace
Of his birth, a new tune sound
For the dance to begin.
For those who live, their blindness gone,
The sight will return of a fruitful earth.
Grasses and clover will bend
Fast in the long wind's race,
Shining like the necks of horses,
Of horses swimming where the sun falls.
And the rose will return to the air
Which once held it and never forgot.

35
BEAUFORT

Beaufort whose cliffs fall sheer a thousand feet
Blots as sun flares the windscreen with bright wings,
Dazzling my eyes, the conqueror springs
Dancing this perfect land's defeat,
Whose smile-like sword is forged in history's heat,
Enemy of stasis, whose hammer rings,
Shattering the images of gods and kings,
Throwing men's small wills before his Master's seat.

For here you'd think brown earth gives all men need
Of food or gods, yet wildness cracks the vacuum
Of self-content as it wrecked shrines and fortresses.
Down gorges I see cars like upturned tortoises
And where they smashed the verge a cross of chromium
Hub-caps mourns the conqueror's newest weapon: speed.

YOUR ONLY NAME

Where differences meet, where water
Touches river banks, where buds
Clench their green in flakes of brown,
Where air slips over, under, wings,
Where seeds rest on the furrowed soil
That frost long softened into tilth,
Where voices in clear air like birds
Wake promise of returning love,
There you are, your only name,
Angel, for making pleasure present
In union of the foreign, joy
In recognition of the strange.

Grey summer clouds move over downs
That move themselves with pollened grass;
And waving with the grasses wave
Girls' locks of hair against the clouds;
They brush it from their mouths in walking,
Their conversation flutes in wind;
Aloft the black kite flies, its twine
Curved to a boy upon the crest:
Your wingtip holds it, bat emblazoned,
Kestrel pillowed on the air,
A cross for man or mind surrendered
To what their natures are when grown.

You haunt me with a sense of what's beyond:
The gravel path curves edge of house,
The lawn sinks out of sight, the beeches,
Voluminous though autumn sounds, repeat
The bosomed shape of cumulus by which
A wedge of starlings wheels, re-forms;
You make death be a word of warmth,
A naming of a shape in time
Life needs to house the light of mind
As skin and form wrap living cells:
Effect of law of seed and fruit
Decreed in quiet of your thought.

And now you give again these downs
In winter pallor browned and green:
Rare-visited bowled valleys,
Springs welling under rounded spurs
Which rise, abut, strike forms upon
The willing mind that gratefully receives
Lost quondams, hidden futures, matrices
That sink impressions into time,
All points from which beginnings can be made,
Coiled codes awaiting replication,
Rich with language, races, songs,
Conserved as limbs of children sleeping.

37
AMBITIONS

To seal the most fugitive essence,
To hear your least murmur or song,
To miss none of the gleams of your beauty
And grow with you, watchful and strong:

These were unspoken ambitions
Made clear as a goldfinch flew
From hedge to an ivy-clung elder,
Escaping my tantalized view.

38
IN THE ROOM OF THE TRIBAL
GODS

1
The light that shapes these figures makes
For sleep.
             I keep
On haunting them as they haunt me;
Their room –
                    an antechamber to the place of dreams –
Holds tactile nightmares, exoskeletons of doom,
Lost ways of dancing, gleams
Of pleasures that we've never known;
And in this season of their lives
When all their tribes are dead as last year's leaves
They bide like over-wintering chrysalids.
But, countering the English light in which they're shown,
About them clings the atmosphere
Of forests where their wood was hewn,
Of nights of movement and of fear,
Where myriads of insects by the foliaged moon
Bombinate and shrill,
And where – imperative and wild
As a stirring of the heart
We have no fantasy or skill
To match or interpret –
In nodding flight
The blue-tailed butterflies dart
Out of undergrowth and are lost to sight
In creepered intervals of trees.

They bring me to the place of waking dreams;
I hear, as much as see, them, set free
In synaesthesia from fear and glower
Of side of night.
                    If they knew their power
O England.

2

Boethius, when Philosophy appeared
Inside your prison cell – her head
Dissolving the vault,
The stars her diadem –
You noticed through your rapture
How tattered were her robes along the hem:
The work of sects who thought they'd capture
The whole
In any rag of truth they stole.

A fable crystallizes in my mood
Seeded by a quiet image:
A sculptor of millennia ago,
His shoulders hunched in concentration on
His own recurring waking dream.
Before him rears a mountain
That speaks and looks at him as though
It were a man or rather all mankind,
So various are its forms and lights.
Delight and terror seize him every time
It slips between him and the day
Until he learns to summon it at will
And by interpretation finds
It draws him to his fate – that he
Should seek its unwrought mass
And make it utter forth, express
The oneness anchoring all the thoughts,
Acts of love, of vengeance, justice
Men picture in the primal nature.
Strong in his vision
He stands in stony squares
Where craftsmen chip;
                          he spoke
Of finding truth in making;
He said that godlike powers awoke

Only in those who like a god created;
And young eyes, fixed on his, shone
At the thought each tedious stroke
Might lose its weariness when awaking
Their self-discovery in the stone.
Wherever he went, his following grew
To seek with him the perfect summit
And when, by travelling far, they knew
No continental range could match his dream,
They built a fleet,
Themselves the shipwrights, themselves the crew,
To bear them past the southern limit
Of islands to the moving sheet
Of landless waters.
                    His gaze
Set their course. A shark's fin
Prodded the horizon's haze.
The white sun swam before their prows,
Dived into shadow, then leapt with ease
To high green alps and swept a blaze
Of light through gulfs that gathered in
Alluvial meadows and the crowns of trees.
He had no need to plan; the island fitted
So well the mountain of his vision,
His plans were all completed.
Full of remembered images
His helpers shared so much his dreams,
Knew how they were interpreted,
They hardly needed supervision
As wordlessly they formed their teams
To cut the spiral road that wound
About the mountain's cone
Up to the guardian peaks around
The caldera of its summit

And from those peaks they hacked the faces
Who, as they looked with love or frowned,
Decreed what theme in wood or stone
Should warm or chill their purviewed places.
Legends of beasts and men possessed
The landykes and escarpment rocks;
Hewn where they stood the trees were dressed
In fearful armies to conquer fear
And endless knots of life snaked out
Through meadows or in mounds enlaced
Mazes at whose centres blocks
Of rough stone shook the finder like a shout.
Beneath the smiling head that threw
Blessings on the island's mildest tract
They built a city like a zoo
Of heraldic monsters.
He died; the language changed; new men read
Differently the words he knew,
Thought God was in the carvings, not the act
Of making, and worshipped them instead.
All carving ceased.
                              One day a joke
Tickled Earth. Her laugh exploded
In a roar of flame that broke
The mountain into halves and hurled
A mushroom shape of god-faced clouds
Into the atmosphere to cloak,
Higher than ever the sculptor's dream had goaded,
The sky with visages in crowds.

These in the winds
Hurtled through dawns and sunsets
Fell randomly,
Dropping fathers,
Dropping mothers,
On pious races
Throughout the world.

It couldn't have happened. It's the chance
That makes them seem the shards and crocks
Of a once united vessel.
Or is it?

3
Numinous they are
And keep the air of love and horror
Felt by those who treasured them,
Who oiled, painted, powdered them, and built
Houses of awe to keep them kind.
They sat
Like spiders in their shadowed lairs
And spun their webs of fear and pleasure
Around their faithful tribes.
But as that power was local,
It could not reach the slaver hold
To calm their chained believers hearing
The corpses tossed to screaming gulls;
Could not deflect the foreign bullets;
Ward off the syphilis, the bibles,
The white-faced men in black
Who waved an image,
Worse than any monster they portrayed,
Of a man nailed to a cross.

Robbed, bartered, betrayed,
Sent here as curiosities
To gather dust in lumber rooms,
They have been rescued by aesthetic piety
To tick together like a bomb.

I could imagine that at night they talk
Each his tribal language. The air
Wails and croaks with syllables that baulk
On blankness and choke in grim despair.
I could imagine through long intercourse
The old forgotten primal code
That works without recourse to words,
Riding through sapless capillaries the road
To activate the field of force
That gives again the power, the choice
Of vengeance
That wrecks the city
And brings back villages
With theirs the ruling voice.

But that's not right –
They deserve more than guilt,
Should be greeted as 'brother'
Be welcomed as 'sister',
They desire not vengeance,
But equal acceptance
In the great recollection
We live through:
Our history.

4

Eyes! we're Sebastians to their glares
Surprised between volleys of their game
Struck by glances, pierced by stares,
Transfixed by knowledge of their aim.
Twin sisters with arms plied round shoulders
Gaze past the face in an unswept wave
Of sea-wrought trunk, wise beholders
Of Birdbeak, solemn as his maker's grave,
Whose headdress loops like damsel-flies
Mating over ponds, back to the head
Of one so drunk with rage his eyes
Of nacre sink below his chest outspread.
Ghosts with green beetle pupils, androgyne
With penis taut and stiffened breasts,
Arouse in us harmonic mental progeny,
Of sound accumulating into crests,
Of humming like demented hives, the sign
Of energy they offer us, the choice
Of ancestry, descent from their great line,
In adding to their own our voice.

5

Within us men and women wait,
Immaculate in heart and love
On mountains where still now the flames
Leap round their summits in the night
To flash on history's wrecks, the art,
Impressions, thoughts that float
Unconvoyed, on collision course,
Across imagination's waves.
They know themselves as golden flames
That roll within their beings, seep
To fire without and love within
In perfect solace of the waking dream,

Know unity within the voice,
The quiet half-heard voice of flame
Whose light is from the life of men
Known in themselves as deeds of love.
Signals of compassion on ourselves.
The flames leap in the wreathing wind.
The wind that guides us, the gust of love
That cuts a gorge across the sea,
That clears a road towards the hills,
Drying the sea-bed at our footsteps,
Carving darts of direction, pointed arrows,
In walls of green water quivering above us.

6
A hand outstretched, a jewel offered,
The lord of dreams permits a sign
Of what the future keeps still coffered
Or deep below the half-sunk mine.
I see a man and woman stand
Naked under thunderclouds, strong
And firm upon a blackened plain. A brand
Of lightning darts and forks a prong
Upon each head. It courses
About their open eyes; then flights
To the heart and round their torsos
In catherine wheels of quick blue lights,
Releasing enzymes, sending blood
Beating with a warm caress,
Awakening in its whirling flood
The chemistry of consciousness;
And to the beat of thunderdrums
The man and woman start to dance.
And, as they dance, a new change comes
As round their feet the lightnings lance
And on their bodies raindrops lash

And stream like flags of many dyes,
Rebounding in a valiant flash
But none more exhilarant than their eyes;
Within their features and their limbs
All races lost without a name
Recover in a subtle glimpse
The ardour of their being, the flame
Of what it was to be themselves
Within this dance of man's rebirth
That lightning wakes as down it delves
To older tombs within the earth.

39

ST SOPHIA: SESTINA

This is a building to listen to; wisdom
Fills it with ghost choirs greeting the Emperor
And voices that answer from galleries of marble,
So vast in its volume of air that time
Preserves in the molecules all patterns of light,
All humming of music that ever broke silence.

Startled at being here, seeing in silence
The dome that ballooned in the legends of wisdom,
I trust to my touch, not eyes or the light,
Finger the monogram of the dead Emperor,
Stroke columns where sunlight on fossilized time
Finds undersea forests in Armorican marble.

Christ the vine is alive in the marble
Of capitals grown in a forest of silence.
It is He who shaped it by entering time:
A model of mind that, echoing His wisdom
Shows man the hemispheres of which He is Emperor,
The world-forming brain He makes conscious of light.

The sacred dances of the court catch light,
The white robes gleam upon pavements of marble
Like reflection of doves round the blood-purple Emperor,
And happy with tears, without this silence,
I never could have guessed mind under wisdom
Veined out so hugely in branches of time.

Space of this order changes life in time:
The mosaic saints burn in the light;
Their sins are smelted to gold by wisdom
Whose greatest miracle, raising stone, brick and marble,
Was to call to its service, to abase with silence
His brothel-reared wife and the demon Emperor.

Crowds round the dome gaze at the Emperor,
Here made Christ's image to mankind in his time,
Where the seraphim pour on him vials of silence
And the eyes of the Virgin in the apse shine with light,
Melting to a mother the Empress of marble
In the church drawn to heaven by the gold chain of wisdom.

We are changed like the Emperor, charged now by wisdom
To speak in our time of the mercies of silence,
Our words born of light, fit for minds cool as marble.